P9-DHI-439

SEEDS OF *Fire,*
ROOTS OF *Hope*

seven principles of inspiration
for the courageous leader

SEES OF *Fire,* ROOTS OF *Hope*

seven principles of inspiration
for the courageous leader

Dr. Jeffrey W. Linkenbach

MILL CITY PRESS
MINNEAPOLIS

Copyright © 2010 by Dr. Jeffrey W. Linkenbach

Mill City Press, Inc.
212 3rd Avenue North, Suite 290
Minneapolis, MN 55401
612.455.2294
www.millcitypublishing.com

All rights reserved. No part of this publication may be reproduced, stored in
a retrieval system, or transmitted, in any form or by any means, electronic,
mechanical, photocopying, recording, or otherwise, without the prior written
permission of the author.

ISBN - 978-1-936400-21-8
ISBN - 1-936400-21-9
LCCN - 2010935112

Cover Design & Typeset by Kristeen Wegner
Printed in the United States of America

CONTENTS

Introduction

Seeds of Fire

*"To properly develop I think
a human being needs guiding principles.
It is from these guiding principles
that we make our decisions."*

Leonard George,
American Indian Chief

More than two decades ago while working as a family therapist, I made a fateful discovery about myself and the people I was serving. My discovery was quite simple in concept but profound in application. What I realized was that in work, as in life, our decisions and actions must be grounded in Spirit. More specifically, I came to understand that to make our lives and our communities work best, we must first stand on a foundation of Spirit before gathering data about what is and planning for action to create what should be. When Spirit leads, everything works better.

Spirit is accessed through reflection. With reflection, we come to identify core principles that provide us with direction and help us discontinue harmful patterns and find deeper meaning in our lives. Through extensive research and application, I identified seven such principles that have become the basis of my work. I didn't realize it at the time, but my own research and reflection set me on a path of discovery that would eventually impact leaders of school systems, agencies, businesses, and universities around the world.

I focused my doctoral studies in adult and community education and began decades of research on the role positive community norms play in helping people go from being busy to being effective, and to ground that effectiveness in meaning. In so doing, I established the National MOST of Us® Institute for Positive Community Norms at Montana State University in Bozeman, Montana.

In community norms research, we gather data from a population not only about people's behavior, but also about the extent to which their behavior is influenced by their perception of how other members of the group behave. Often, perceptions are incorrect. Due to a variety of factors, we tend to misperceive the positive norm; that is, the goodness that surrounds us, or the positive choices already being made by the group. These misperceptions are problematic because they erode the fabric of trust that is the essence of community. Once revealed, however, the positive norm can be used to educate people and influence their actions in a constructive manner. Positive data tends to make more of a difference in people's lives than negative data or communications based on fear. This precept serves as a foundation to the leadership principles presented in this book, for *the Positive* is the first step to bringing Spirit into our communities and work groups.

As leaders, we are called upon to inspire others to create meaningful change. Now and again, we must champion efforts to reform an agency, transform limiting social patterns into greater health, respond to sinking profits, or guide a major business re-structure. These processes are ingrained in our vernacular as leaders, yet in practice transformation is an uncomfortable and sometimes challenging process. In order to make and sustain meaningful change, we must reorganize the way we think and communicate – starting with a shift in the way we perceive what's going on around us.

Transformation, as daunting as it may seem at times, is well worth orienting our lives to. In fact, it's essential. With our modern day focus on work; all of our busy-ness and often corresponding emptiness – with an unprecedented need and opportunity in our communities and the global economy for connection and collaboration – it has never been more important to become heartfelt leaders. By humbly attending to our deepest desires and transforming our perceptions and behaviors, we can learn to lead purposeful lives and help communities achieve their potential.

Fundamentally positive and health-centered in its outlook, this approach to leadership pulls from different normative theories a variety of methods that can be used to correct negative misperceptions and to identify, model, and promote positive behaviors that are the norm in a group or organization. This approach is a blueprint for transformation used by leaders to cultivate a sense of Spirit that guides evaluation and decision-making in an effort to improve outcomes.

To create lasting change that reflects what we really want for ourselves, we must start with Spirit. We need something bigger than ourselves to guide us in determining which information is important and which behaviors to choose going forward. This may be a soulful calling such as we experience at other times in our lives – in the wilderness, at church, in the love we feel for a family member – and hunger for in our working lives as well. What we long for is there and calls to each of us; its essence will call to us in various ways until we respond. Transformational leaders know and seek this. This Spirit of Leadership, if you will, can be found in the Seven Guiding Principles.

Getting the Most Out of the Seven Guiding Principles

By reflecting upon and applying the Principles presented in the following chapters, we experience hope, truth, and the contagious energy of shared inspiration, because:

1... Being Positive is our natural state.
2... Being Present allows us to live in the only reaity that exists – the Now.
3... Being Perceptive honors what is right and good in people as well as community.
4... Being Purposeful brings hope, as we align our intentions with transformation.
5... Being Perfected we acknowledge we are learners in progress.
6... Being Proactive means we choose what we give attention to.
7... Being Passionate directs us towards serving others.

Each Principle chapter presents insights for contemplation and practice. These truths function as energy sources to help focus and inspire us from a larger perspective so that our actions are properly directed. At the end of each chapter, you'll find an exercise that asks you to apply the Principle internally (perception) and externally (relating to others) by reflecting on questions and writing a bold, claiming statement about the Principle as it relates to your life.

There are many ways to bring the reflections to life in work or personal activities; they can be used as a guide for leadership teams or vehicles for self-directed or guided contemplation. Here are just a few of the ways individuals and groups have used the Principles and reflections:

- Choose a reflection and journal about how it applies to you or your work.
- Structure your day with reflections: each hour, choose a reflection to peruse, pause, and ponder – how does the statement speak to you in this moment?
- Read and reflect upon the introduction to each chapter.
- Randomly open the book and read a reflection, then ask yourself: how do I resonate with this idea?
- In a group process, when stuck – stop, pull out this book, and read one of the statements. Pause to "listen inside," and make a comment about why that statement is appropriate for you or

your group right now. When you resume your work, you will have shifted the energy.

- Review the Principles and ask yourself whether there is a place in your life where you're stuck, and on which Principle you feel in your gut you should focus. How do you resonate with that Principle? Reflect on some of the statements.

- Use the Principles to guide the development of your leadership team: if building the Principles into leadership team principles or values, systematically go through them to find areas of commonality. Alternatively, have your team choose one Principle to discuss as it relates to your work. Or, use them in consultation with the development of your leadership model.

- In times of conflict or resistance, stop and talk about which statements you agree on. Higher truths are places of agreement. Bigger picture truths are tools for facilitating connection and community.

While the Principles are presented in a specific order, it is nevertheless appropriate to skip around and read them in a non-linear manner. At the beginning of a new initiative, the presented order tends to be most useful, but once you become familiar with the Principles, you will know what flow works for you and how best to use them. There is a wisdom to the presented order, but listen to your internal compass.

We are all called upon to be leaders because we are all called upon to serve others in some way. Ultimately, the answers we seek are found in the experience of community; we are social beings who derive meaning and purpose within the context of our relationships to others. That is, our dedication to becoming more engaged and productive individuals is realized and purposefully expressed in community. In our desire to make a difference, we sometimes forget that the solutions to our challenges already exist in the communities where we live and work. This is the foundation of this model – that we don't bring sustainability into the room with us, it was there before we arrived. There is an incredible goodness in community waiting to be uncovered and directed. To do this, we often need only a way to regain or maintain a larger perspective – of Spirit, of our authentic selves, of the meaning of service. My goal with this book is to bring this hope forward and to help you allow its energy to express itself. To this end, the Principles provide a path, a clarity; they help us step back, connect with what really matters, and to *think from our hearts*. When we think from our hearts, everything else falls into place.

J.W.L., September 2010

SEVEN PRINCIPLES OF INSPIRATION
FOR THE COURAGEOUS LEADER

One
Be Positive

Key Assumption: Being Positive is our natural state.

The Positive is our natural state. It's who we truly are underneath layers of painful life experiences in response to which we created defenses and protections. These protections are real, but they were created under conditions that no longer reflect our reality. To be Positive, then, is to shed our protections in the now and live our truth – to identify and claim who we really are.

How we respond to the existence of the Positive within us and others directs our lives: either the Positive is experienced by us (hope, acceptance, love, forgiveness), or it is not (fear). Our common quest as individuals, communities, and cultures is defined by how effective we are at directing the positive energies of our lives or, conversely, how busy we become constructing diversions from the truth that we are Positive.

Daring to look deeply, we must confront our greatest fears, which are not about death or loss, but rather about living. What we fear the most is a life transformed by the knowledge that the Positive exists within us.

To be Positive is a daring adventure of facing and then living out the goodness that exists within ourselves, and accepting the tremendous responsibility we have to serve the needs of others. The Positive is the spirit of hope and community that we all share. Deep down, we all know that irrespective of our temporary conditions, we have everything we need to better ourselves, our organizations, our cultures, and our world. It is through the Positive that we can do this.

1. The Positive does not ignore life's problems, but instead provides a practical approach for experiencing freedom by looking deeply into each situation and making conscious decisions to co-create a more positive reality.

2. When you enter a new community, it is critical that you realize the Positive is already there. Begin your work by claiming, "There is good in this place."

3. It takes more effort to accurately perceive the Positive in a situation than it does to passively join the misperceptions of a negative culture.

4. Trust establishes the necessary foundation for transforming any organizational system or relationship. When trust is absent, fear and inaccurate interpretations multiply.

5. Fear promotes exclusion. Community spirit is one of inclusion.

6. Your role as a leader is to encourage and direct dialogue. Wise leaders facilitate the balance between honoring the reality of people's pain, and channeling the conversation toward healing and hope.

7. Authentic dialogue is necessary for transformation: When in doubt, speak your deeper truth because you never know who is listening – including yourself.

8. In your efforts to create healthier groups and cultures, remember that the Positive transforms lives, one perception at a time.

9. Effective leaders dare to see the tiniest seed of the Positive in every situation because they know it has the power to transform everything.

10. Wise leaders realize the Positive is always present and understand that their primary job is to make this reality more visible to others.

11. You know you are transforming a situation when your "I/Thou" distinction becomes blurry. The conceptual boundaries between you as observer, and those you are serving, disappear.

12. Rest in the knowledge that you will experience the wisdom you need in any situation.

13. Great leaders create the conditions for authentic dialogue as a tool for promoting the Positive.

14. Learning to perceive the goodness in others creates the healing loop you have been seeking in yourself.

15. Turn down the volume! It's hard to perceive deeper peace when your mind is generating so much noise and static. In the Positive, there is a lot you can let go of.

16. The more resistance your mind generates in order to avoid seeing that the Positive is the deeper reality, the more suffering you continue to cause for yourself and everyone around you. It takes tremendous energy to continue manufacturing fear.

17. Communicate from your positive intent. Words are powerful, so keep them positive.

18. Realize that what you say about "the culture" is what you see in yourself.

19. The communities you serve already possess everything they need to heal themselves.

20. Communicating the Positive is not about saying the positive things people want to hear; it's about seeking and speaking our authentic truth.

21. It is impossible to create comprehensive solutions from deficit-based thinking where something is always lacking. We find solutions by living in the Positive.

22. Wherever you go, peace is already there. Your challenge is to accurately perceive this presence and co-create positive outcomes.

23. Stillness is helpful in recognizing the Positive that resides in your soul.

24. Genuine forgiveness is at the root of all spiritual transformation. It is through this process that we dissolve the misperceptions that give root to our fears, judgments, insecurities, and faulty interpretations.

25. Empathy and the courageous experiencing of our pain and sadness is always a substitute for negativity.

26. As you strive to perceive things as they really are, you are re-writing history. You will notice changes in the stories you tell.

27. At our core, we yearn to see things as they really are. The problem is that we could spend a lifetime avoiding this simple truth by gathering data to support our fears and misperceptions.

28. If we allow ourselves to believe we are separate and disconnected from other people, nature, and Spirit, we promote fear.

29. Our capacity to inspire and lead others is a direct reflection of our dedication to living the Positive.

30. When you slow down your mind by focusing on the Positive, you will hear the song of your soul. Don't rest without letting this song out into the world today.

31. The Positive leader can walk into any problem situation and perceive a deeper calm operating below the surface illusion of turmoil.

32. Dedicating ourselves to the Positive is about learning to see and honor the positiveness in every other person.

33. Perceptual literacy is not about ignoring problems and pain, but doing the exact opposite – daring to go deeply into those places and see things as they really are in order to transform them.

34. Transformation does not occur by constantly focusing on the elements impeding change. You cannot back into greatness.

35. Wise leaders view the totality of a situation and withdraw resources that contribute to problem perceptions. There is a wisdom in parting ways with ideas and projects that obscure the Positive.

36. Living from within the Positive promotes mental, emotional, spiritual, and physical health. Promoting the Positive should become part of national health policy – the core of universal coverage.

37. Don't underestimate the tremendous need that all of us share to connect around a positive story that is bigger than ourselves.

38. It is your responsibility to create the more positive reality in the world that you see underneath the surface.

39. One of our most common misperceptions is that life is static. When we recognize that our organizations and communities are constantly shifting, we position ourselves to influence the direction of change towards the Positive.

40. Misperception begins by forgetting who you really are at your core. Remember who you are in your natural state – this is the path to the Positive.

41. Acknowledge the deep roots of your fear, but then look underneath your fear to perceive the life force that can melt terror. This is true courage and the way of positive leadership.

42. Your effectiveness as a leader involves developing the skills of framing – re-inserting positive context into stories, and speaking in ways that create a more holistic view of who we are.

43. The greatest gift we can give others is the hope that they can transform the world.

44. There is an incredible readiness in the world for the emergence of the Positive. People are ready to hear and tell a new story and that story must begin with you.

Internal	• How I think about myself • How I treat myself • How I view others	• How our organization sees itself as a part of community • How we interact with each other

Principle #1
Be POSITIVE

Positive: Characterized by or displaying affirmation or acceptance; involving advantage or good.

Guiding Questions

1. *What are some truths about your positive nature?*

_____

2. *What are some positive "I Am..." statements about you?*

_____

3. *How are you successful at directing positive energy?*

_____

4. *How will you increase "the Positive" in your life?*

_____

5. *How can you improve the direction of positive energy in your life to better serve others?*

_____

Write a bold statement that claims and establishes Core Principle #1, Be Positive:

_____

_____

"Transformational leaders learn to reject old hypotheses in their quest for deeper truth."

Seeds of Fire, Roots of Hope

• How I perceive others • How I treat other people • How I interact with my community and the world	• How our organization interacts with the world • How our organization serves community	External

Principle #1
Be POSITIVE

Positive: Characterized by or displaying affirmation or acceptance; involving advantage or good.

Guiding Questions

1. What are some truths about being positive with others?

_____

2. How will you direct positive energy toward others?

_____

3. How can you benefit others by becoming more positive?

_____

4. How can your organization better achieve its mission by being more positive?

_____

5. How would that better the lives of others?

_____

Write a bold statement that claims and establishes Core Principle #1, Be Positive:

_____

_____

"Our capacity to inspire and lead others is a direct reflection of our dedication to living the Positive."

Seeds of Fire, Roots of Hope

Two
Be Present

Key Assumption: Being Present allows us to live
the only reality that exists – the Now.

The Present is the only reality that exists. By focusing our attention on the Now, we work with what is, not what was or what might be, creating a readiness for transformation to occur. The positive wholeness that we all long for is not found in a re-interpreted past or a romanticized future – it is only found in the here and now.

Directing attention to the Present is important because the Present is where all of the answers to life's mysteries are immediately accessible. We are often tempted to create an illusion of certainty, sidestep our suffering, and control the unknown by focusing on the past or the future, and shutting down the potential for transformation. Life's conditions are always moving and changing, but only in the Present can we access truth and the Positive.

Creating the space for the Positive to emerge in the Present involves courageous language and authentic dialogue. Honoring people's experience in the Present – not asking them to be someone else for the sake of our own comfort – co-creates conditions of hope, courage, and the willingness to receive the goodness that is here and awaits discovery. Be real right now – it's the best you can do.

Reflect on these statements to be in the Present:

1. Transformation only happens in real time.

2. There are many things that medicate us from experiencing the pain of the present, such as misperception, fear, control, addictions. Paradoxically, it is only by being fully present with this pain – taking a deep, courageous look into it – that we transcend it.

3. You cannot change your current perceptions in the future. You either do it now or perhaps not at all.

4. Your ability to accurately perceive a deeper reality in any situation is highly correlated to your ability to be Present.

5. Transformational leaders are committed to growth now because they realize that the answers are fleeting.

6. You experience the Positive by realizing that it is right here, right now, in the Present.

7. The first step in any transformation is to accept things just as they are and not how you would like them to be.

8. At any time, you can choose to shift your reality by choosing to see the world and others differently.

9. The only way to create a positive outcome in your future is to transform your perceptions in the present.

10. We must learn to slow down the present, sometimes putting our brains on pause, to stop from living out patterns of the past and see something new.

11. You create your destiny moment by moment by perceiving exactly what you expect.

12. Our readiness to serve and lead others is first and foremost related to our own internal calm. All of us have conflicting thoughts and feelings inside our heads that can dissipate our strength. Inside our heads is a crowded room full of people who are all talking at once, striving to be heard. However, when you choose to focus on what is true in the present moment, Spirit enters the room and all of these competing voices are silenced and standing at attention to the importance of where you are about to direct them.

13. Positive thinking is a byproduct of placing your attention onto the Present.

14. By owning the consequences of your actions today, you are making room for enlightenment tomorrow.

15. Communities and organizations whose leaders delay experiencing the Positive until some future conditions are met will notice other leaders emerging. The Positive always finds a way to manifest in the Now and vice versa.

16. Seeing the deeper truth in any situation is possible when you practice accurately perceiving what is going on within and around you, moment by moment. Looking into the present moment is what allows you to accurately see things as they really are.

17. The Positive is always present here and now. Any thoughts to the contrary are misperceptions from the past.

18. If you want different results in your life and work, you must learn to see the world differently by re-directing your thoughts toward what is happening inside you at the present moment.

19. Take a mental vacation by breathing into the infinite goodness that surrounds you at this very moment.

20. All of the joy, meaning, and wellbeing that you desire in your life are yours for the taking if you create that reality in the present moment. Stop looking for it tomorrow.

21. If perceptions of your current situation are not bringing you peace and freedom at this very moment, consider that it is not the conditions of your situation that need to change but rather your perceptions.

22. Children live the positive reality in each moment. They have much to teach us if we would just listen.

23. You have everything you need to experience joy in this moment if you take time to see things as they really are.

24. At every moment, you can choose to perceive the world and people in ways that support happiness and success instead of ways that do not.

25. You may think professionalism is about a well-groomed exterior, but in reality everything you perceive is always on display.

26. Absolutism is a mental retreat from the path of enlightenment. Growth is a process of moving through all the ambiguity of the Present.

27. Waiting to experience big miracles in life can be a form of spiritual escapism. By waiting for the lottery to call your number, you are missing the millions of micro-miracles that you are co-creating all around you in every moment.

28. Forgiveness is a process that results in changing your perceptions in the Present. Anger and resentment come from the past and are superimposed on the future. Ask yourself, "Why am I avoiding the Now?"

29. Carpe See-Em: *Seize What You Sees!*

30. Avoiding interpretation is a process of living in the present moment, and this experience always leaves you transformed.

31. It is instructive to watch yourself choose your perceptions minute by minute, breath by breath. You always learn something new.

32. Being Present in the Now can be the difference in moving from feeling tired to feeling inspired.

33. Each day, each hour, each moment, the world hands you opportunities of a lifetime. Your job is to recognize and act upon them.

34. Transformation in ourselves and the communities we serve comes from experiencing accurate perceptions of who we are in the present moment.

35. Wise leaders monitor their perceptions of the person they are talking to so that they can dissolve thoughts of separation that appear as competition, prejudice, judgments, and preconceived notions. If we are present, we are listening, not talking to ourselves.

36. Through stillness you can perceive the presence of the Positive working in your life.

37. When we misperceive the Present, we make stories up about the situation by placing negative experiences about the past onto the Present.

38. You do not correct misperceptions by focusing on them, but by shifting attention to the emerging positive truth of the moment.

39. It is critical that you speak your truth now – even if it is going to be misperceived by those listening. Remember, you are also listening.

40. When you feel stuck, direct the conversation toward the Positive in the Present moment and notice how a clear vision begins to emerge.

Internal	• How I think about myself • How I treat myself • How I view others	• How our organization sees itself as a part of community • How we interact with each other

Principle #2
Be PRESENT

Present: Existing now or in progress, being in view or at hand.

Guiding Questions

1. _Describe how it feels when you are living in the present._

_____

2. _What benefits do you experience by being present?_

_____

3. _How can you increase your capacity to be fully present?_

_____

4. _How can learn from the past and plan for the future and still be in the present?_

_____

Write a bold statement that claims and establishes Core Principle #2, Be Present:

_____

_____

"You experience the Positive by realizing that it is right here, right now."

Seeds of Fire, Roots of Hope

• How I perceive others • How I treat other people • How I interact with my community and the world	• How our organization interacts with the world • How our organization serves community	External

Principle #2

Be PRESENT

Present: Existing now or in progress, being in view or at hand.

Guiding Questions

1. How will being present affect how you relate to others?

_____

2. What does it mean to be present with your community?

_____

3. In what ways can you better serve others by increasing your ability to fully experience the present?

_____

4. How is being present a key to being an effective leader?

_____

5. How can your organization be more present?

_____

Write a bold statement that claims and establishes Core Principle #2, Be Present:

"At any time, you can choose to shift your reality by choosing to see the world and others differently."

Seeds of Fire, Roots of Hope

Three
Be Perceptive

Key Assumption: Being Perceptive honors
what is good in people and community.

Perception is everything. What we perceive to be real is
what we create in our lives and in the world. The way we
perceive something solidifies it as that – whether or not
it is an accurate reflection of what is really there. This is
why perception is so important.

Perception is the misty interface in consciousness between the human trinity of our thoughts and feelings,
actions, and our deeper spiritual self. Through attention
and effort, we can develop our perceptual abilities to
see the deeper existence (reality) of the Positive in every person and situation. Thus, we can choose how we
perceive something. This unique human characteristic of
being able to choose what and how we perceive is the
existential freedom and responsibility that enables us to
co-create positive outcomes for ourselves, our organizations, and cultures around the world.

As perception is everything, so too is misperception. Often times we bring information in through a lens (formed
by past experiences) of fear, distrust, judgment and so
on, which creates misperception. Thus, being perceptive
is an active process that also involves correcting misperception, the root source of all problems, pain, and suffering.

Positive transformation requires true humility, which is to acknowledge our tendency to err in what we perceive to be real. We must resist using our maps to define the territory of what's real, because our maps don't necessarily reflect what exists as real today. The misperception of disconnection – from self, others, the earth, God – is a core misperception based upon fear that triggers more fear and which also, in turn, perpetuates misperception. Instead, we must choose to perceive the deeper truth; that is, the Positive in ourselves, others, and what happens around us.

The following insights will help you develop accurate perception:

1. Human beings can transform their lives and the world around them by changing their perceptions.

2. Misperception extracts energy and produces fatigue.

3. When you focus on perceiving wholeness, all of the things that are not wholeness become glaringly apparent.

4. All misperceptions arise from fear, creating more fear.

5. Your mind manufactures misperceptions, but your heart can see the reality of things as they truly are.

6. Investing energy into negative perceptions demonstrates the law of diminish-
   ing returns. Listen.

7. Perception is everything; so, too, is
   misperception.

8. Accurate perception is the first step in
   solving any problem.

9. If you are not sure about what you perceive, then work backwards by looking
   at your actions – they will always be in
   alignment with your perception.

10. All new initiatives come in colorful at-
    tractive packages, but wise leaders per-
    ceive the difference between form and
    substance.

11. Watch how quickly your brain jumps to
    conclusions and interpretations about
    what you see. Then hit reverse and no-
    tice everything you just missed.

12. You are always just one positive percep-
    tion away from altering your future and
    re-writing your past.

13. To live deeply and honestly, you must
    look and listen to others, not just your
    perceptions of them.

14. Accurate perception of any situation always helps you overcome fear with hope.

15. All of us are capable of perceiving things as they really are.

16. There is always a deeper unshakeable calm residing underneath the busy surface waters of misperceptions.

17. Personal reflection is the process of surveying your perceptions by comparing your current outdated beliefs with the emerging reality of the present moment, and then consciously taking time to upload this more accurate data into your thoughts.

18. At any given moment check your perceptual balance sheet by asking yourself, "Am I investing more energy into defending my current views than I am into learning new ones?"

19. Positive thinking is a byproduct of positive perceptions.

20. Irrespective of the discomfort you may be experiencing, transformation is only a perception away.

21. The best coaches, consultants, spiritual guides, and therapists cannot facilitate a transformation in how you perceive the world if you are not ready to do so. Humility is being willing to see things differently.

22. As a leader, you need to have the discipline to correct your misperceptions so that you don't pass negative thinking on to those you work with.

23. Spirit knocks at the door of your belief system. If you answer, you will see things differently.

24. Accurate perceptions are achieved through a humbling process of not believing everything you think.

25. Accurate perceptions of the Positive are only possible when you see the reality that you are connected to everyone else.

26. The moments when you become aware of your ability to choose your perceptions are the moments when you have the power to determine your future.

27. It is critical to distinguish between the noise in your head and the noise coming from your environment.

28. How you lead others is more a reflection of your perceptual habits than your formal education.

29. Positive perceptions can overcome negative facts. This is how hope works: First we believe, then we see.

30. When we are at war inside ourselves, we will passively perceive the need to create external conditions that foster conflict.

31. Seek a deeper truth within yourself and your misperceptions will fall away by themselves.

32. Your body never lies; deeper truth always resides in your body. Learn to go there for wisdom about what is needed from you.

33. Accurate perceptions of other people always result in greater feelings of love and compassion for them. If you feel anything else, you are seeing them through the eyes of negative projections.

34. Most people are so accustomed to associating themselves with their misperceptions that they do not even realize they are constantly choosing the world they see. Transformation begins when you notice what you are attending to.

35. It's amazing how quickly people in your life change when you begin to take responsibility for your perceptions of them.

36. Change your language by using only positive terms and words, and observe how you perceive the world in a more positive way.

37. Enlightenment comes by observing how you observe. Notice the micro-second between events in the outer world and how quickly you attach meaning to them.

38. How do you know if you are accurately perceiving a situation? Ask yourself this question: Right now, am I emptying myself of my own interpretations and creating space to see the Positive in others?

39. When you do not know how to proceed with a decision, it is often because you are misperceiving yourself as too small to handle the challenge. Look beyond yourself by recognizing that your actions are part of a larger whole and you will see more clearly how you should proceed.

40. Perception 101: Where you place the energy of your attention will expand. This law applies to both love and fear.

41. Notice how you promote factionalism and the need to divide and conquer when you perceive yourself as powerless against threats. Use this energy as a clue that you need to transform your perception in relationship to others. Community is always a choice.

42. Slow down your thinking by focusing on what is happening inside and around you. At this moment you have synchronized your energies with your life's purpose.

43. Value the down times in your daily schedule. Through times of silence, you have the opportunity to perceive a deeper reality.

44. Noticing the sacred space between your perceptions and your thoughts is a skill you must practice in order to transform your life. Spirit lives there!

Internal	• How I think about myself • How I treat myself • How I view others	• How our organization sees itself as a part of community • How we interact with each other

Principle #3
Be PERCEPTIVE

Perceptive: Capable of exhibiting keen perception, observant.

Guiding Questions

1. *What is the relationship between transforming your own perceptions and your wellbeing?*

_____

2. *How can you be more aware of your perceptions?*

_____

3. *What happens when you misperceive versus when you accurately perceive?*

_____

4. *How will you correct your own misperceptions?*

_____

Write a bold statement that claims and establishes Core Principle #3, Be Perceptive:

_____

_____

"The accurate perception of any situation you face always helps you overcome fear through hope."

                                        Seeds of Fire, Roots of Hope

• How I perceive others • How I treat other people • How I interact with my community and the world	• How our organization interacts with the world • How our organization serves community	**External**

Principle #3
Be PERCEPTIVE

Perceptive: Capable of exhibiting keen perception, observant.

Guiding Questions

1. How can your organization raise its perceptive capacity?

2. What is the role of correcting misperceptions in being an effective leader?

3. How will misperceptions in the community affect you?

4. What role does transforming misperceptions play in your organization's mission?

5. How will a perceptive culture help your organization?

Write a bold statement that claims and establishes Core Principle #3, Be Perceptive:

"How you lead others is more a reflection of your perceptual habits than your formal education."

Seeds of Fire, Roots of Hope

Four
Be Purposeful

Key Assumption: Being Purposeful brings hope,
as we align our intentions with transformation.

When we are Purposeful, we bring positive results into
our own lives and hope into the lives of others. We create
what we truly seek in our lives by aligning our intentions
with positive transformation.

To be Purposeful is to be inspired by the potential of the
future, not pushed or driven by the past. By consciously
choosing positive intentions, we know exactly how to direct our speech and actions to manifest the Positive in
the next moment. Life has great meaning, and it is bigger than ourselves. By being Purposeful we can learn to
bring the Positive into being.

We all share a common purpose in yearning to experience authentic community; after all, it is only by serving
others that our deepest meaning can be realized. Self-
transformation is vital, but incomplete. The hero's journey involves service. Being Purposeful means choosing a
positive intention.

Use these reflective statements to be Purposeful:

1. Our perceptions are self-fulfilling prophesies. With purpose, we can choose ones that align with what we desire.

2. Your job is to invest in transforming your life. The rest is simply detail.

3. If your purpose is more about serving others than about serving your ego, you will build organizational systems that outlive you.

4. The most critical element of understanding your perceptions or misperceptions is how they serve your purpose.

5. You were not born to just exist or struggle through each day. Remember who you really are. Seek a more expansive purpose in your life.

6. Beware of the seduction of funding which lures you into producing data and views that support a purpose that is self-serving rather than transformational.

7. Every perception and misperception serves a deeper purpose, which is revealed by your thoughts, words, and actions. Seek a purpose that honors others.

8. You will experience increased energy when you are accurately perceiving and acting according to your life's purpose.

9. It is impossible to accurately perceive the truth of your situation while simultaneously investing energy into protecting a certain paradigm.

10. What is the value of having insights if you are not applying them in the service of others?

11. Most of the obstacles in your life are self-created as a result of the misperception of your deeper purpose for being.

12. Living with purpose requires perceiving on purpose.

13. One of the most common human errors is to identify yourself with your thoughts, feelings, and attitudes. You are so much more.

14. Become a leader who dares to breathe in the fire of hate and exhale words of hope.

15. When we create dichotomies we push purpose out of the equation.

16. Look deeply into that subtle feeling of angst and dissatisfaction you often feel but put in the background of your life through busyness. It is your soul that is patiently waiting to show you how to see things differently.

17. Your thoughts, feelings, and actions always serve your perceptions. Choose wisely where you focus your attention.

18. Dedicate yourself to seeing things as they truly are and you will find your life's purpose.

19. Are you promoting the illusion of deficit or the reality of wholeness in your interactions with other people?

20. When you focus on watering the seeds of fear, you strengthen the roots of separation – in yourself and in the world. Yet, when you spend your day cultivating purpose of love, peace and connectedness, negativity dissolves as you create the reality you are nurturing.

21. If you seek to become a leader who transforms the world, you must free yourself from being defined by how others see you. Dare to be authentic.

22. The tendency to avoid fully seeing problems and pain as they really are is the basis of all our emotional illness, disease, human suffering, and political strife.

23. The journey of 1,000 miles does not begin with a single step; it begins with orienting oneself in the proper direction.

24. People with positive perceptual intelligence turn fear into a power that serves others through hope.

25. Wise leaders do not present absolute doctrine. They understand that purpose must be aligned with a great cause.

26. Meaning, fulfillment, and purpose are wonderful byproducts of dedicating yourself to seeing things as they really are.

27. The purpose of a life characterized by a dedication to the Positive is an increased capacity to serve others.

28. A positive work ethic is the direct result of perceiving purpose in everything you do. Paradoxically, it then stops feeling like work.

29. Behind your thoughts, feelings, and actions, you will find your perceptions. Continue to look deeper and you will find the purpose your perceptions serve. Go deeper still and you find your place in community.

30. When you operate from a place of purpose, you feel compelled and driven. Accurate perceptions of a situation result in being pulled by the future more than pushed by the past.

31. If someone's non-verbal energy is not positive, listen to her advice with caution. Re-frame a higher purpose before proceeding.

32. We default to the paradigm of war when we have not invested our resources into the difficult work of transforming toward community and seeing the situation for what it really is. This is the true hero's purpose.

33. Take heart – the destiny of your ego is to disappear into a deeper service of others. When this is your purpose, nothing can stop you.

34. Fears will continue to arise in your life. Your purpose is to transcend your current level of thinking and rise above these illusions.

35. Your life's purpose is found by turning inward and daring to transform the misperception that the truth you are seeking resides outside yourself.

36. Dedicate this day to aligning your words with your convictions and you will perceive the significance of your life differently. Choices become clear.

37. Wise leaders frame information in ways to serve higher purpose and not their misperceptions.

38. Your purpose in life is to expand your internal capacity to love others by transforming the way that you see the world. Start here and all of the other details will fall into place.

39. Your ego's main purpose is survival and demands that you tenaciously cling to your misperceptions of a threatening world. Your Spirit's main purpose is to thrive, which only occurs as you dare to trust in a power greater than your ego.

40. Freedom is terrifying, so we create misperceptions about our soulful purpose as distractions from facing our deeper existential journey toward greatness.

Internal	• How I think about myself • How I treat myself • How I view others	• How our organization sees itself as a part of community • How we interact with each other

Principle #4

Be PURPOSEFUL

Purposeful: Having a purpose or aim, full of determination.

Guiding Questions

1. What is your purpose in life?

_____

2. How will you structure your time and energy to focus on your purpose?

_____

3. How is your life purpose connected to serving others?

_____

4. How will your purpose manifest in service?

_____

Write a bold statement that claims and establishes Core Principle #4, Be Purposeful:

_____

_____

"Your job is to invest in transforming your life. The rest is simply detail."

Seeds of Fire, Roots of Hope

• How I perceive others • How I treat other people • How I interact with my community and the world	• How our organization interacts with the world • How our organization serves community	External

Principle #4

Be PURPOSEFUL

Purposeful: Having a purpose or aim, full of determination.

<u>Guiding Questions</u>

1. How can you continue to align your life purpose with the mission of your organization?

---

2. How will you increase your capacity to better serve others?

---

3. How will you align your purpose with the purpose of others?

---

4. How will your organization's purpose transform to better serve community?

Write a bold statement that claims and establishes Core Principle #4, Be Purposeful:

"What is the value of having insights if you are not applying them in service of others?"

Seeds of Fire, Roots of Hope

Five

Be Perfected

Key Assumption: Being Perfected acknowledges
we are works in progress.

To be Perfected is to understand we are in a process of transformation, moving toward wholeness and community. The path to being Perfected is through humility – the critical skill of consciously choosing to dissolve our limited views in dedication to seeking a deeper reality. We need the courage to be imperfect in order to be made more whole. Having the courage to claim that we are works in progress always results in a greater sense of connectedness to self, Spirit, nature, and others. In fact, transformation requires such an acknowledgement.

These insights will help you have the courage to be Perfected:

1. All of us have the capacity to positively impact the world if we learn how to first transform ourselves. Dare to be imperfect.

2. Have you ever noticed how some theories of change never evolve? Dedicate yourself to the process of transformation and fresh ideas will come to you.

3. Transformational leaders approach problems with questions rather than answers.

4. Accurate perceptions – daring to see things as they truly are – is the humble hero's journey that we must all embark upon.

5. Identifying others' misperceptions is easy. Seeing yourself for who you really are – now that is work.

6. Your willingness to correct misperceptions in yourself is directly related to the positive impacts you will have on other people.

7. Our universal human quest is to find wholeness. Great leaders understand this as a process of courage, humility, and life-long learning.

8. Wise leaders surround themselves with people who are dedicated to seeing and speaking about things as they really are. Weak leaders prefer the presence of people who agree with their views.

9. The beginning of all transformation is daring to experience your ignorance.

10. The only theory of human behavior that is truly sustainable is one that constantly re-invents itself.

11. Your will to transform is established when your desire to change outweighs your pattern of clinging to old misperceptions.

12. If the theory underlying your work has not evolved, it has become dogma and is an obstacle to your growth and to that of those around you.

13. Transformation is not something you abandon after you have achieved success and stability. It is an ongoing dedication to life itself.

14. It is essential that you learn to approach each conversation with an openness to how the other person holds a key to how you can further transform yourself.

15. If you are not fully aware of the positive and negative impacts your organization's culture is having upon others, you can be assured that the universe will provide you with ample opportunities to experience them firsthand.

16. Even organizations whose mission is to bring healing and social justice promote harm when they cling too tightly to their own ideologies and beliefs.

17. True humility is demonstrated through a daily practice of seeking truth because you come to understand that the current views you possess are not absolute and changeless.

18. It's not just what you see that matters, but what you do about what you see.

19. The more you see the world through the dominant patterns of your mind, the longer it will take you to experience the power of the Positive manifesting in your life.

20. Society loves to promote the illusion of deficit – that there is a missing part of you out there that, once found, will make you feel whole. Meanwhile, the truth about your current wholeness waits patiently.

21. A major byproduct of practicing forgiveness is that you transform your misperceptions – of yourself, other people, and the cultures around you. Forgiveness allows you to experience the peace you have been seeking.

22. Seeing a deeper reality is a dynamic process of moving your attention to create balance, which then requires additional movement. Being Perfected allows you be a work in progress.

23. The second act of transforming your misperceptions involves having the courage to act upon your newfound insights. Social action and self-growth are symbiotic.

24. Dare to be Perfected if you are not seeing the effects of the Positive transforming your life in tangible ways.

25. After we have experienced being transformed through a renewal of our perceptions, we must continue to practice positive thinking in order for it to become solidified in our lives.

26. Transformation occurs when we dare to perceive things outside of our patterned way of interpreting information. The more that we practice going to our places of ignorance, the easier it becomes.

27. I know that I am seeing things as they really are when I no longer see myself as "the consultant" and others as "clients." This distinction becomes blurred as all of us are being transformed by co-creating a more positive reality. Being Perfected promotes community.

28. It is impossible to stand for social justice while harboring negative thoughts about others. You will deplete the energy of your soul.

29. Breathe deeply and create space for Spirit to deepen your most treasured beliefs. Make room to become bigger than you are.

30. Forgiveness is one of the most profound transforming agents of all time. True forgiveness is not just about changing how you view the other person, but about transforming your views of yourself. It does not change what has happened, but it does change your perception so that you see your hurt in a new way.

31. Develop the courage to be "good enough." Being Perfected recognizes that we are never perfect. Waiting for perfection is self-serving when the world needs you NOW.

32. Your wisdom as a leader requires you to learn the skill of deeply listening to people with whom you disagree. Solutions to complex problems require your ability to acknowledge multiple truths in order to find common ground. This is seeking community.

33. It is dangerous to think that the knowledge you currently possess is the absolute truth. Have the courage to recognize your imperfect way of perceiving the world.

34. Personal transformation is required if you want to genuinely lead others. It is not some optional elective in a management seminar, but lies at the root of effectiveness. Your capacity to accurately perceive how to impact others is directly related to the integrity of your inner work.

35. Quit letting your fear of future challenges get in the way of trusting Spirit today. Of course more will be expected of you, but you will not be the same person facing those challenges. If you think about it, most of your self-created problems are the result of resisting this process of being Perfected.

36. The process of transformation is not about becoming perfect. Life will still demand that you identify and neutralize negative energy. However, through practice, you become more adept at sensing and steering clear of negative situations.

37. Your character and influence as a leader can only expand at the rate at which you accept your imperfection and transform yourself.

38. The way you perceive yourself in one area of your life affects your entire life. For example, it is impossible for you to perceive yourself and people at work in ways that do not affect your relationship to your spouse or children. Being Perfected is a process toward wholeness, in which all the parts of our lives our connected.

39. If you are not getting the results you seek – greater peace, connections with others, sound sleep and wholeness – then you are spending too much time thinking and not acting from courage.

40. The most inspirational and effective leaders have the courage to be imperfect.

41. If you read these words and say, "There is nothing new here," you are correct. These truths are ancient. The question is how are you applying them in your daily life?

Internal	• How I think about myself • How I treat myself • How I view others	• How our organization sees itself as a part of community • How we interact with each other

Principle #5
Be PERFECTED

Perfected: To bring to final form, to make perfect, improve, refine.

Guiding Questions

1. _How can you improve your acceptance of your flaws?_

_____

2. _How can your calling to serve others allow you to be courageous enough to model imperfection?_

_____

3. _What role does humor play in being imperfect?_

_____

4. _How are authenticity and trust connected to having the courage to be imperfect?_

_____

Write a bold statement that claims and establishes Core Principle #5, Be Perfected:

_____

_____

"Identifying others' misperceptions is easy. Seeing yourself for who you really are – now that is work."

Seeds of Fire, Roots of Hope

• How I perceive others • How I treat other people • How I interact with my community and the world	• How our organization interacts with the world • How our organization serves community	External

Principle #5

Be PERFECTED

Perfected: To bring to final form, to make perfect, improve, refine.

Guiding Questions

1. _How will being imperfect affect how you relate to others?_

_____

2. _How can an honest examination of your imperfections allow you to increase capacity in your organization?_

_____

3. _How will your organization model a learning culture?_

_____

4. _How can you use fear and ego as guides in your development as an imperfect leader?_

_____

Write a bold statement that claims and establishes Core Principle #5, Be Perfected:

_____

_____

"The most inspirational and effective leaders have the courage to be imperfect."

Seeds of Fire, Roots of Hope

Six
Be Proactive

Key Assumption: Being Proactive means
we choose what we give our attention to.

To be Proactive is to actively choose where we place our attention and what actions we will take. By noticing what is happening – reactions both inside and outside ourselves – we transcend reaction, and can instead choose whether and how to respond to our circumstances. This process produces an experience of hope; we trust ourselves within the natural ebb and flow of life without having the illusion that we need to be in control. When we misperceive or fail to trust, we need to be in control because we're afraid reality is determined by what happens outside ourselves.

Being Proactive is critical because it is only with awareness of our reactions and the limits of our current thinking that we create room to see a deeper reality. We can be Proactive by consciously choosing to look beyond the boundaries of our current paradigms, which are always based on past circumstances.

By watching our own expression of thoughts, feelings, and actions – and perceiving them without judgment – we experience a new reality. By experiencing this new reality, we are able to see how to best act (or not act) in order to positively impact others. Positive transformation is an active, not a passive or reactive process.

These reflective statements will help you be Proactive:

1. Perception is not merely a thought process but an action, because what you choose to focus on will grow and expand in your life.

2. Wise leaders invest in transforming their inner cultures because they understand that the outer world always conforms to the inner world.

3. Don't focus on correcting misperceptions in others at the expense of promoting accurate ones in yourself. Being Proactive is about both of these processes.

4. Look deeply into a situation so that you can determine if it is time for reflection or time for action. Being Proactive is often non-active.

5. Contemplate your deepest convictions. What you believe directs what you perceive, which determines your reality.

6. Wise leaders act to remove everything that is not aligned with their vision of a positive reality. Being Proactive demands clarity of vision.

7. You must dare to see that it is your most
    trusted paradigms that are keeping you
    from experiencing a deeper reality. Be-
    ing Proactive feels risky.

8. Understand that by creating conditions
    for people to focus on and speak a deep-
    er truth, transformation is happening.

9. If you allow your last thought of the day
    to be about perceiving tomorrow in a
    new way, you will succeed in doing so.
    This is proactive sleeping.

10. It is important to speak each sentence as
    though it were a piece of art that you are
    placing your signature on – because you
    are.

11. Welcome to leadership: You are now re-
    sponsible for communicating the world
    you perceive.

12. Transformational   leaders   understand
    that their role is to create conditions that
    allow the Positive to manifest.

13. Transformation is a byproduct of proactive work — it requires that you make a conscious effort to see a deeper truth trying to emerge in each situation, rather than lazily misperceiving surface-level illusions.

14. Choose your words carefully, because you will begin to see and believe the things you hear yourself say to others.

15. When you focus on problems, you are manifesting deficit thinking. Proactive leaders see and speak about wholeness.

16. Don't buy into the passivity of the cliché that "everything in life happens for a reason." Everything happens for an infinite number of reasons, and you get to co-create what they are.

17. Environments of hope dissolve misperceptions and fear.

18. Great leaders recognize effectiveness, not busyness. Today, are you busy or are you effective?

19. If you don't have a plan for how you will positively focus your day, there are plenty of people who will direct you.

20. More money does not improve community health when it is invested in focusing on the problems in that community. Proactive leadership invests in a vision of community health working.

21. Once you learn the skill of differentiating between positive and negative perceptions in your life, you must discipline yourself so that you choose the former.

22. You will become what you think about all day long. Choose to focus on the Positive.

23. Wise leaders see every situation through a proactive lens and dare to re-write history.

24. Leaders must act despite ambiguity, picking up cues along the way. You know if you are accurately seeing things when the results of your actions become lucid. Doors open, teachers appear, and the environment says, "This way."

25. One of the greatest problems with modern leadership models is that they are often based upon reducing deficiencies rather than sharing power. To become a more effective leader you must think differently by seeing positives when others refuse to do so.

26. You know you are leading your organization well if you are in dialogue with other viewpoints that do not support your own.

27. Reflection is not some passive luxury, but the hard work of a true leader.

28. The process of accurate perception is proactive, not passive. Accurate perception is choice in action.

29. Commit this day to aligning your words and actions with the deeper stirrings of your soul and tomorrow things will look different.

30. The saying that 'the truth is the first casualty of war' also applies to our domestic social wars. Proactive leaders see conflicts in their mind as opportunities for promoting community.

31. Reaction is the evidence of misperception. Pro-action is connected to the Spirit of a deeper truth.

32. In order to increase your leadership and influence on others, you must develop a greater capacity to observe toxic situations without compulsively reacting to them.

33. It takes tremendous courage to accurately perceive and act to create the Positive in every situation.

34. If you don't like the answers you receive to the questions you ask, then maybe you need to ask different questions. Always asking what is wrong with yourself and others is tiring and gets old quickly. Proactive leaders change the world by asking about what is right and good.

35. One of the keys to transforming your life through your perceptions is to observe and change your language. The power of language, like all transformation, is hidden in paradox. We do not talk about the world that we perceive; we see the world that we talk about.

36. Being Positive and Proactive in life is not about pretending everything is wonderful when it is not. It is about learning how to observe life from a neutral position and then choosing how to act to make each situation better.

37. Inspiring more positive, accurate worldviews in other people is not so much about presenting them with right facts and statistical data as it is about motivating them to take action by redefining the stories of their lives.

38. Proactive leadership, by definition, is "upstream" thinking. You must learn to quickly move your attention from the problem "upstream" to the headwaters of the solution.

39. If you want to become more effective in your leadership, create environments filled with positive energy and avoid situations where people are invested in over-focusing on problems.

40. Accurate perception of your current life situation is a process of relaxing into the deep positive presence in your life, rather than merely convincing your mind to work harder.

41. Before you quit your current job, transform your thinking as if you were going to stay there forever. Then, you will be worthy of serving your next position.

42. Busyness is the enemy of effectiveness. When we are busy, we default to our comfortable patterns of perceiving. It is only by slowing down our lives that we can begin to focus attention on transforming the way we interpret and process information.

43. Staying busy is the most socially acceptable form of passiveness and ineffectiveness. It avoids the hard work of transformation.

44. It is critical that we transform fear into hope and anger into compassion if we want to be effective leaders. Leadership is courage in action.

Internal	• How I think about myself • How I treat myself • How I view others	• How our organization sees itself as a part of community • How we interact with each other

Principle #6
Be PROACTIVE

Proactive: Acting in advance to deal with an expected difficulty; anticipatory, to look or plan ahead.

Guiding Questions

1. How will you increase your ability to be proactive?

_____

2. How will being proactive bring more calm to your life?

_____

3. How will you plan your actions from a place of neutrality?

_____

4. How will you structure time to reflect?

_____

5. How will you move from being busy to being effective?

_____

Write a bold statement that claims and establishes Core Principle #6, Be Proactive:

_____

_____

"Wise leaders see every situation through a proactive lens and dare to re-write history."

Seeds of Fire, Roots of Hope

• How I perceive others
• How I treat other people
• How I interact with my
  community and the world
	• How our organization
	  interacts with the world
	• How our organization
	  serves community
		External

Principle #6
Be PROACTIVE

Proactive: Acting in advance to deal with an expected difficulty; anticipatory, to look or plan ahead.

Guiding Questions

1. How will you be proactive (i.e., non-reactive) with others?

_____

2. How will you help others to be proactive?

_____

3. How will you help your community be proactive?

_____

4. How will the quality of your proactive thinking better serve your organization and its mission?

_____

5. How can your organization be more proactive?

_____

Write a bold statement that claims and establishes Core Principle #6, Be Proactive:

....

....

"Reaction is the evidence of misperception. Proaction is connected to the spirit of a deeper truth."

                                    Seeds of Fire, Roots of Hope

Seven
Be Passionate

Key Assumption: Being Passionate directs us
toward serving others.

To be Passionate is to unleash the wild and meaningful life our souls desire and be in the moment-to-moment flow of connectedness to others. It is to live out and share with others the energy of being Positive and the gift of being alive.

Becoming more passionate in our growth towards the Positive is one side of the human equation, but a self-help focus is not enough to sustain us. We must also direct our passion toward serving others in order to be whole. It is impossible to create positive transformation in our individual lives without also directing our attention toward positively impacting others, and vice versa. True enlightenment, and the enthusiasm of transforming a more positive life, must always express itself in community. Being Passionate is about directing the energy of self-transformation into the act of serving others.

Use these reflections to be Passionate:

1. Perceive life with awe and humility. Now
    go take on the day!

2. Notice how your positive perceptions immediately produce increased energy, peace of mind and improved health. Sustain these feelings throughout the challenges of your day.

3. Your freedom lies in having the courage to challenge your most cherished ideas in the quest of serving others.

4. Observe the difference in how you perceive the world after you say, "Yes, but ..." compared to when you say, "Yes and ...".

5. Transforming perceptions is not merely an intellectual process of learning how to think differently, but a complete metamorphosis that results in more passion and more calm.

6. Transforming perceptions is a process of reclaiming power: Not a power over other people, but the true power of serving them through deeper understanding.

7. Transformational leaders dare to leave their fear of failure behind in order to manifest a reality that is bigger than themselves – one they know they could never control.

8. Accurate perceptions will connect you to spiritual energy and vitality.

9. Promoting positive perceptions is a reciprocal agent of healing: what goes out to others comes back through you in the form of passion.

10. You will know if you are accurately perceiving the truth of a situation if the byproducts of your views produce freedom, joy, compassion, acceptance of others, and a deep calm that surpasses your need to act or speak.

11. Allow yourself the privilege of deepening your connection to the mysteries in ordinary days that cannot be fully explained with words.

12. Accurate perceptions always liberate, whereas misperceptions constrict. Your body will show you this truth.

13. Passion is contagious and spreads from your courageous action to bystanders who are fearfully standing on the sidelines, waiting for their name to be called. Have the courage to call out to them.

14. Take time to notice that when you touch one strand of positive reality in yourself, it is always connected to a massive hairball of good things.

15. When two people come together by sharing misperceptions, their symbiotic bond is temporary. But when people connect through a Spirit of community, they have touched something eternal.

16. For today, speak only positive words to yourself and other people and perceive the healing effects of what you speak coming back to you.

17. When you cling tightly to the false security of your current belief system, your misperceptions serve your distorted need to avoid the unbridled ecstasy of being alive. Dare to unleash your passion – and serve!

18. Great leaders transform themselves through regular times of reflection, contemplation, and meditation. Passion is a byproduct of these activities.

19. Take a walk with a child and learn how they perceive the world. Then go imitate this on your own. Don't worry, when you get stuck and forget how, they will eagerly show you again.

20. The key to effective leadership is forging a well-worn path into the calm place of your soul. Then, when you face ugly situations, you know how to proceed with lucidity.

21. Look deeply into your fear of success and you will dissolve your misperception that you must journey alone.

22. The way of Spirit feels like woo-woo to the scientific mind, and the way of science feels like confinement to Spirit. But action that serves others is a bridge that melds these together without duality.

23. Practice positive perceptions every day, because this is the key to spreading joy in yourself and others.

24. Evidence of the Positive working in your life is when you accurately perceive the extraordinary within ordinary happenings.

25. You know you are making progress when you notice that the private conversations in your head have moved from fighting evil to embracing goodness.

26. The essence of leadership is to inspire others through the courageous example of transforming our own lives.

27. Your capacity for inspiring other people expands as you transform your fears into hope.

28. The most common misperception of today's leaders is to assume their job is to motivate others. Motivation is always external and fleeting. Lasting change comes through the passion of a transformed life, which means seeing things differently and experiencing positive impacts.

29. Evidence of personal transformation is seen when your need for staying in your calm place outweighs your need to convince other people of your worldview.

30. Practicing positive perceptions inspires you to serve others with passion. How great is that?

31. The degree to which we positively impact people we have contact with is directly proportional to the level of mastery we have over dedicating ourselves to the Positive.

32. The internal challenge you face as a leader is not about developing another strategic plan or comprehensive program. Of course you must. But the real challenge is to infuse your program with passion so that it can be most effective.

33. When you water the seeds of the Positive that already exist inside the deepest parts of your being, you will be transformed and experience a new-found passion for life.

34. The problem with mindlessly communicating half-truths is that you will see and believe the things you say. Speak truth, even if your voice shakes, and your passion will give you courage in how to proceed.

35. Courage is always about making your life and other lives better. Fear masks itself as fighting problems instead of solving them. Passion is an outcome of daring to live from this distinction.

36. The antidote to powerlessness in life is to focus on serving others, because when you do so, you view yourself and the world differently. Moving attention from yourself to others is the great circle.

37. The true benchmark of an accurate perception is how much it benefits others. Their energy and passion will tell you if you are on course.

38. Your transformation is not just about you. You have a responsibility to live life more fully.

39. Seeking accurate perceptions as an organization or community does not mean that everyone will see things the same way. That would merely be uniformity. Accuracy in perception is about honoring individual views and building broad coalitions.

40. Don't expect other people to launch parades and fireworks when you have spiritual epiphanies. Your rewards are silent and personal. Channel your passion into social action.

41. Great leaders inspire. You are a great leader. Now passionately seek out opportunities to serve.

Internal	• How I think about myself • How I treat myself • How I view others	• How our organization sees itself as a part of community • How we interact with each other

Principle #7

Be PASSIONATE

Passionate: Capable of, affected by, or expressing intense feeling.

Guiding Questions

1. *How can you connect your passions with your calling of service to others?*

_____

2. *How do you nurture your passions?*

_____

3. *How can you allow more passion into your work in order to increase your positive energy?*

_____

4. *How can you incorporate daily habits that foster your passion for life?*

_____

Write a bold statement that claims and establishes Core Principle #7, Be Passionate:

_____

_____

"Practice positive perceptions every day, because this is the key to spreading joy in yourself and others."

Seeds of Fire, Roots of Hope

• How I perceive others
• How I treat other people
• How I interact with my
  community and the world
	• How our organization
	  interacts with the world
	• How our organization
	  serves community
		External

Principle #7

Be PASSIONATE

Passionate: Capable of, affected by, or expressing intense feeling.

Guiding Questions

1. How can your organization improve as a community of support and renewal?

_____

2. How is the passion in your organization the lifeblood of sustaining things that matter?

_____

3. How can your organization inspire others?

_____

4. How can your organization provide leadership by celebrating the goodness that exists in your community?

_____

Write a bold statement that claims and establishes Core Principle #7, Be Passionate:

....

....

"Great leaders inspire. You are a great leader. Now passionately seek out opportunities to serve."

                            Seeds of Fire, Roots of Hope

Epilogue
Roots of Hope

As leaders, we inspire transformation – it's who we are and what we do – and the Seven Core Principles provide a bridge for us to advance to the next level of our journeys. Over the past decade, I have been fortunate to be a part of projects in several non-governmental organizations, community health organizations, corporations, and state and federal agencies. In Wyoming and Minnesota, for example, leaders from health departments and local community coalitions attended one of our workshops to learn how to use the Seven Core Principles in framing, speaking about, and planning on project issues. Bringing Spirit into leadership has contributed to yet other successes:

- *A school district in a small Native Alaskan fishing village*. In this setting, the Core Principles were used to integrate the spirit of the entire community into how the school district directed and presented itself. The superintendent recognized that the wishes of the entire community needed to be honored by becoming an integral part of the school's persona. It was critical that the district developed a positive set of guiding principles because the community was experiencing significant depression and negativity as a response to issues of poverty and the influences of alcohol on many families.

- *A corporate occupational health and safety organization representing 3.3 million service workers and 83,000 businesses across Ontario, Canada.* Here, the principles were used to develop executive team leadership goals and a communications framework. After this work, the company CEO came to Montana for a Science of the Positive™ "boot camp" – an onsite visit where, over three days, she focused on the spirit of transformation in leadership, the science of planned change, and actions to implement best practices. As a result, the CEO sent key leaders to Montana to go through the same process so as to align her executive team with these Core Principles.

- *A major federal agency, for development of a strategic communications process built upon the Seven Core Principles.* Expert researchers and practitioners from across the nation utilized the Core Principles to help create a positive communications framework and guiding leadership principles for discussing critical national health issues.

What I have noticed over the past two decades of studying and applying these Principles is that when people are successful, it is because they have learned to appreciate the adventure of discovering how *the Positive* is unfolding in their lives. An extensive literature base exists on strategies for conducting surveys and market testing to support change. But the paradox of Spirit reveals how 'non-technique' creates the conditions to produce the results we traditionally seek through technique. The primary technique of this work is focusing on the journey itself, an adventure of individual and collective transformation. When we as leaders are growing and are excited about the discoveries of our own lives, it shows up in our work as we model and invite others to join. The Positive is contagious!

There is tremendous freedom in knowing that the solutions organizations and communities seek to their problems already reside within these entities. By grounding our work in Spirit, we experience hope, inspiration, and the healing energy of community. The more we apply these principles to our work, the more we experience a widening of our circle of influence and support. This upward spiral of positive energy is the essence of transformation and why so many leaders are planting Seeds of Fire and growing Roots of Hope.

Engaging in the process of positive transformation is about daring to see things as they really are in order to embrace the unknowable future with the intention and willingness of believing something wonderful is about to happen. We have seen this trustworthy inspiration come alive in many communities and organizations. I am confident that it will come alive for you too.

Acknowledgments

While this book is my own creative expression based upon many years of work, it merely represents one way I add my voice to a chorus of community. I have had the great honor of applying these transformational principles with colleagues who dare to challenge and support themselves and our clients as we venture from the mysteries of spirit into the practicalities of science. A deeply felt thank you goes out each day to Diane Hipp, Jerry Evans, Kelly Jutila, Harvey Wolfe, Katie Zientara, Anu Sharma, Roger Svendsen, Deb Strachan, Sarah Keller, Darren Lubbers, Pam Tindall, Gary Lande, and Doug Young: You inspire me. Although he would never want to be singled out, I must say a special thank you to Jay Otto.

For clients to become partners in daring to apply these principles in leadership demonstrates a special trust, and to them I am humbled. Thank you all.

Editing a book like this one is so much more than technical. Thank you Lisa Upson for how you combined your own soul with your talents and craft.

I am most grateful for the people who bring my life daily meaning and joy: Cindy, Christopher, and Annika.

About Jeffrey W. Linkenbach, Ed.D.

Jeffrey W. Linkenbach, Ed.D. is an internationally respected social entrepreneur and founder of The Science of the Positive™ framework of transformation.

Jeff is a Senior Research Scientist with and Director of the Center for the Study of Health and Safety Culture at Montana State University, where he also founded and directs the National MOST of Us® Institute for Positive Community Norms. His expertise and technical assistance are frequently sought by leaders of communities, colleges, public schools, private foundations, corporations, and government agencies who strive to implement science-based solutions. His clients have included the U.S. Centers for Disease Control and Prevention, Harvard University, and the American Medical Association.

As a dynamic speaker, consultant, and educator, Jeff inspires leaders to achieve profoundly meaningful results in both their individual and organizational lives. His award-winning work impacts millions of people around the world through proactive community leadership. Using a timeless combination of Spirit, Science, and Action, Jeff demystifies the process of transformation and provides a practical blueprint for achieving it – one that is both effective and fulfilling.

Jeff lives in Bozeman, Montana with his wife, Cindy, and their children, who bring meaning and purpose to his work and life.

CPSIA information can be obtained at www.ICGtesting.com
261363BV00001B/1/P

9 781936 400218